Lerner SPORTS

ALL-STAR SMACKDOWN

LAMAR JACKSON VS. CAM NEWTON

WHO WOULD WIN?

KELLEY BARTH

Lerner Publications ◆ Minneapolis

The stats and information in this book are accurate through the 2024–2025 NFL season.

Lerner Publications Company
An imprint of Lerner Publishing Group, Inc.
241 First Avenue North
Minneapolis, MN 55401 USA

For reading levels and more information, look up this title at www.lernerbooks.com.

Main body text set in Aptifer Sans LT Pro.
Typeface provided by Linotype AG.

Library of Congress Cataloging-in-Publication Data

Names: Barth, Kelley author
Title: Lamar Jackson vs. Cam Newton : who would win? / Kelley Barth.
Other titles: Lamar Jackson versus Cam Newton
Description: Minneapolis : Lerner Publications, [2026] | Series: Lerner Sports. All-star smackdown | Includes bibliographical references and index. | Audience: Ages 7–11 | Audience: Grades 2–3 | Summary: "Lamar Jackson and Cam Newton are two of the most electric players in NFL history. But who would win in a head-to-head matchup. Read about the greatest moments and key stats. Then, decide for yourself!"—Provided by publisher.
Identifiers: LCCN 2025011530 (print) | LCCN 2025011531 (ebook) | ISBN 9798765689455 lib. bdg. | ISBN 9798348028398 pbk | ISBN 9798765694343 epub
Subjects: LCSH: Football players—United States—Rating of—Juvenile literature | Quarterbacks (Football)—United States—Statistics—Juvenile literature | African American football players—United States—Statistics—Juvenile literature | Jackson, Lamar, 1997– | Newton, Cam, 1989– | Sports rivalries—United States—History—Juvenile literature | LCGFT: Statistics
Classification: LCC GV939.A1 B368 2026 (print) | LCC GV939.A1 (ebook) | DDC 796.332092/2—dc23/eng/20250605

LC record available at https://lccn.loc.gov/2025011530
LC ebook record available at https://lccn.loc.gov/2025011531

Manufactured in the United States of America
1 – CG – 12/15/25

TABLE OF CONTENTS

Cam Newton

INTRODUCTION

FOOTBALL LEGENDS

In January 2016, quarterback Cam Newton and the Carolina Panthers were facing the Arizona Cardinals. It was the conference championship, and the winner would go on to play in the Super Bowl.

FAST FACTS

- Cam Newton won the Offensive Player of the Year award in 2015.
- Newton holds the National Football League (NFL) record for the quarterback with the most rushing touchdowns.
- Lamar Jackson is a two-time NFL Most Valuable Player (MVP) winner.
- Jackson holds the NFL record for most career rushing yards for a quarterback.

Less than two minutes were left in the first half. The Panthers were only one yard away from the end zone. Newton held onto the ball and leapt over the huddled players. He stretched his arms across the end zone and scored.

The Panthers won the game 49–15. Newton had plenty to be proud of. He threw for a total of 335 yards and two touchdowns. He also rushed for 47 yards and two more touchdowns. Newton and his team were headed to the Super Bowl.

Lamar Jackson

Five years later in 2021, quarterback Lamar Jackson and the Baltimore Ravens were playing the Indianapolis Colts. Things looked bad for the Ravens. They were down 9–22 at the end of the third quarter. But then the team came alive. Jackson threw for back-to-back touchdowns. They eventually tied the score 25–25. The game went into overtime, and Jackson threw a touchdown pass to win the game.

It was the game of a lifetime for Jackson. He rushed for 62 yards. He also threw four touchdown passes and a Ravens team record 442 yards. He set a new league record by completing 86 percent of the 40 passes he threw during the game.

Newton and Jackson are both record-breaking quarterbacks. But who would win in a head-to-head matchup? Let the smackdown begin!

Cam Newton (center) celebrates the Carolina Panthers' NFC Championship win in 2016.

Lamar Jackson is known for both his elite passing and rushing.

CHAPTER 1

Newton reacts to the cheering crowd during the 2010 Southeastern Conference championship game between Auburn and South Carolina.

JOURNEY TO GREATNESS

Cam Newton was born on May 11, 1989, in Atlanta, Georgia. School and sports were both important in the Newton household. His passing skills and ultra-fast speed got the attention of many top college football programs.

Newton's college career got off to a bit of a rocky start. He faced injuries and changed schools a few times. But by his junior year in 2010, Newton was the starting quarterback for Auburn University. Newton helped his team win the

Southeastern Conference championship with a score of 56–17. Newton threw for a total of four touchdowns and ran for two more. One of these touchdowns amazed the crowd.

Newton threw a deep 51-yard pass into the end zone just before the end of the first half. The ball grazed off an opponent's fingertips. But Newton's teammate caught it for a touchdown.

That year, Newton helped Auburn win the national championship. He won the AP College Football Player of the Year award. He also won the Heisman Trophy, an award given

Newton shows off his rushing skills during a game for Auburn University.

each year to the best college player in the country. Newton decided to turn pro. In 2011, the Carolina Panthers picked him in the NFL Draft.

Lamar Jackson was born on January 7, 1997, in Pompano Beach, Florida. Jackson's mom recognized her son's talent early on. She started practicing with him in the backyard. Her coaching and his hard work paid off. Jackson showed off his smart playmaking in high school. He went on to play football at the University of Louisville.

Jackson started showing a talent for football in elementary school. He could throw a football 20 yards by the time he was eight.

Jackson looks to throw during a 2016 game for the Louisville Cardinals.

By his second year of college, Jackson was putting up big numbers on the field. In the first game of the season, he threw and ran for a total of eight touchdowns before halftime. That season, Jackson threw for 30 touchdowns. He also rushed for 21 touchdowns. He led his team to nine wins that season.

Jackson also won the Heisman Trophy that year. He was the first player from the University of Louisville to win the award and the youngest Heisman winner of all time. Jackson continued to build on his success. He threw for a total of 3,660 yards and rushed for 1,601 yards the following year. In 2018, he joined the Baltimore Ravens.

Jackson won the Heisman Trophy in 2016 and was a Heisman finalist in 2017.

CONSIDER THIS

Newton and Jackson were both first-round draft picks. However, Newton was the first overall pick of the 2011 NFL Draft. Jackson was the 32nd pick in 2018—the last pick of the first round.

Newton holds up a Carolina Panthers jersey after being picked first in the 2011 NFL Draft.

CHAPTER 2

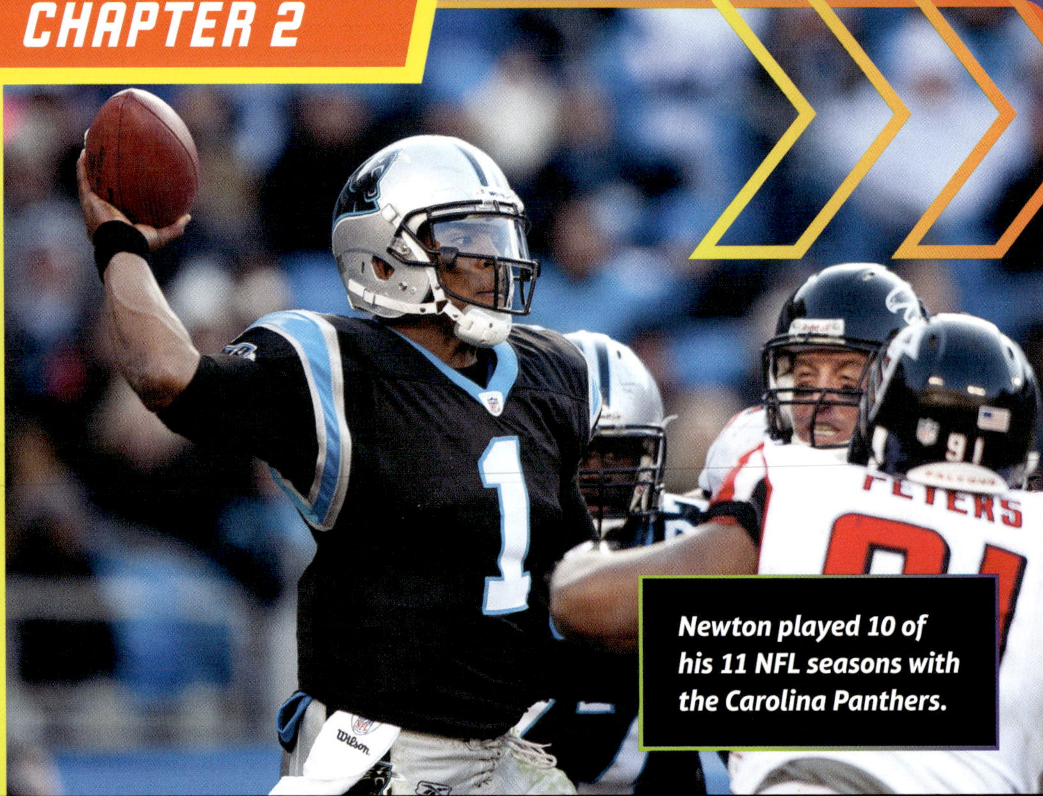

Newton played 10 of his 11 NFL seasons with the Carolina Panthers.

GREAT MOMENTS

Cam Newton got off to a record-breaking start in the NFL. He threw for 422 yards in his very first game. This set an NFL record for most passing yards in a quarterback's first game as a pro. Even though the Panthers ended the season with six wins and 10 losses, Newton had a lot to be proud of. He won the Offensive Rookie of the Year award. He also had 14 rushing touchdowns, a new NFL record at that time.

The 2015 season was a great one for Newton and the Panthers. They ended with 15 wins and only one loss. It was the best season in team history. Newton scored 45 touchdowns and led all quarterbacks in rushing yards and rushing touchdowns. He was named league MVP and won the Offensive Player of the Year award.

Football fans were impressed by how much Newton improved year after year. In 2015, he led his team all the way to the Super Bowl. But the Panthers' offense didn't have a good game. After an interception, two fumbles, and seven sacks, the Panthers lost to the Denver Broncos 24–10.

Newton scrambles out of the pocket during a 2015 game against the Atlanta Falcons.

CONSIDER THIS

Newton and Jackson have proven their leadership skills on and off the field. Jackson runs a charity called Forever Dreamers. Their goal is to teach people about children's mental health. The Cam Newton Foundation was formed in 2012 to help children in need.

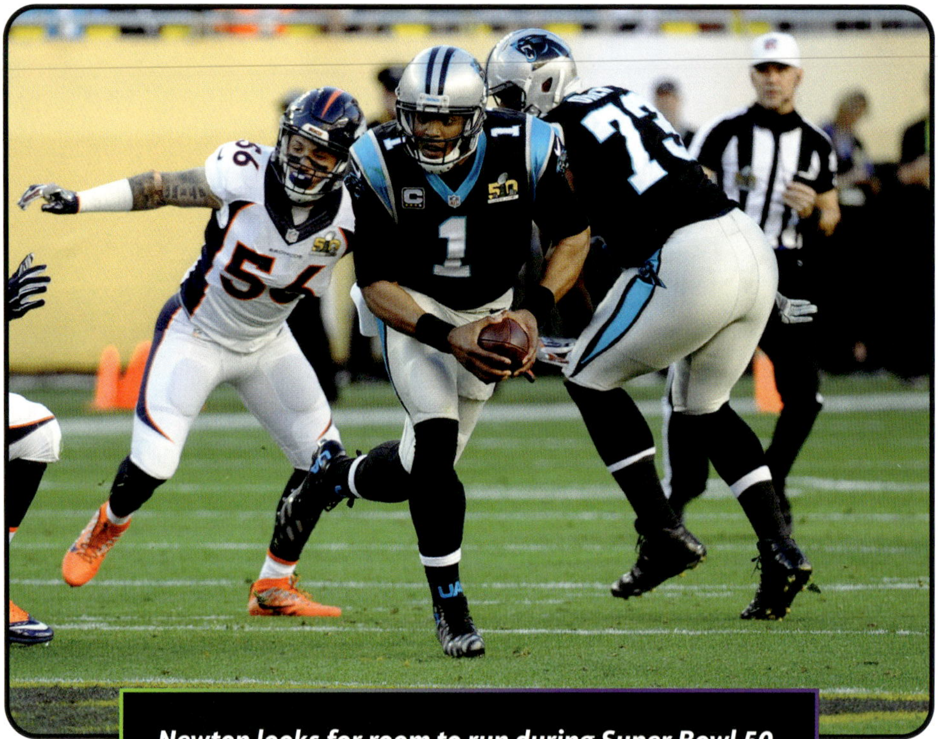

Newton looks for room to run during Super Bowl 50.

Lamar Jackson didn't begin his 2018 rookie season as the starting quarterback. But when quarterback Joe Flacco was injured, Jackson stepped into the starting role. With Jackson as quarterback, the team won six games and lost only one.

Before the next season, the coaching staff built a team that would best support Jackson's inventive style of play.

The next year, Jackson led the Ravens to a 14-win season. In a late-season game against the New York Jets, Jackson ran the ball eight times for a total of 86 yards. That brought his season rushing total to 1,206 yards, an NFL quarterback record.

Jackson looks for an open receiver in a 2019 game against the Cleveland Browns.

Jackson wasn't just the best rushing quarterback in the league. He had the sixth-most rushing yards of all players, including running backs. Jackson also led the league in touchdown passes and had the highest rating of any quarterback. It was no surprise when he won the NFL MVP award.

Jackson holds his second NFL MVP trophy in 2023.

Jackson passed for 36 touchdowns in 2019, earning his first NFL MVP award.

Four years later in 2023, Jackson had another excellent season. One memorable moment happened in the conference championship game. Jackson threw a pass, but it was knocked into the air by the other team. The ball was loose, which meant the other team had a chance to intercept it. But Jackson didn't let that happen. He ran forward and caught his own pass for a gain of 13 yards. That season, Jackson won his second MVP award.

CHAPTER 3

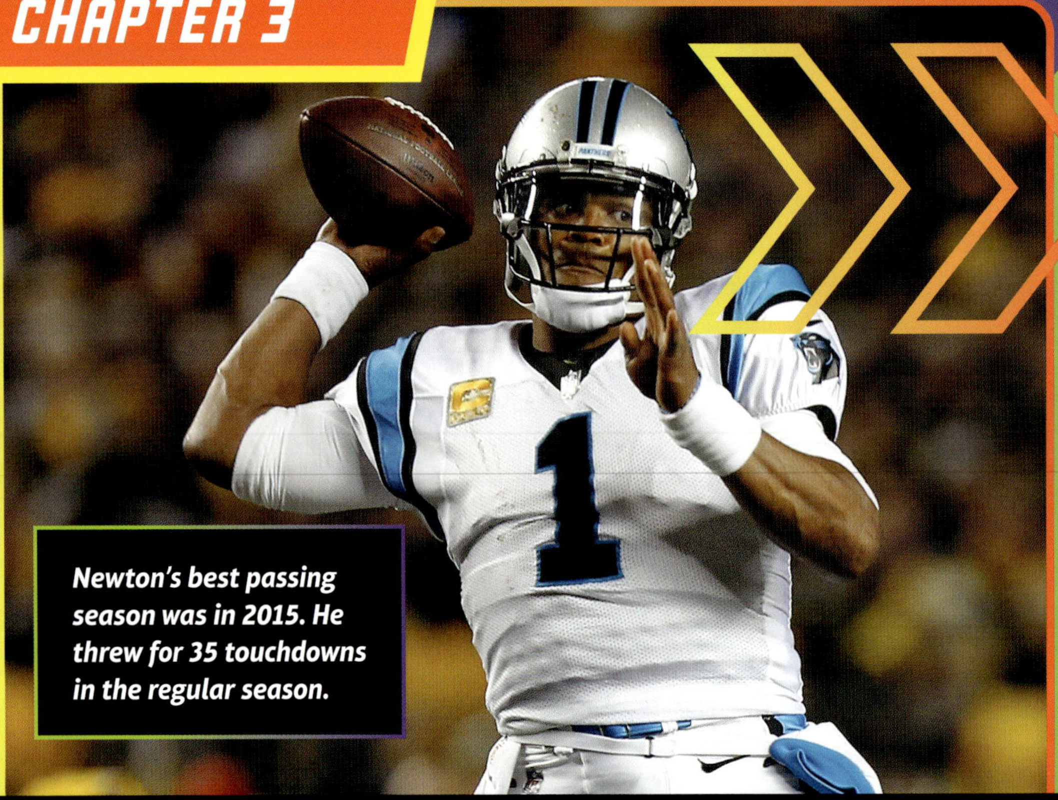

Newton's best passing season was in 2015. He threw for 35 touchdowns in the regular season.

ALL-STAR QUARTERBACKS

Newton and Jackson are fantastic quarterbacks. They are both considered dual threats who can throw and run the ball at a high level. Newton played in the NFL for 11 years in 148 regular-season games. He successfully threw the ball almost 60 percent of the time.

Jackson has played in the NFL for seven seasons and has played 103 regular-season games so far. He has completed almost 65 percent of his throws. On average, Newton threw for more yards per game. But Jackson scored more touchdowns per game.

Both quarterbacks hold NFL records for their rushing ability. Jackson holds the record for most career rushing yards for a quarterback with 6,173. In 2019, he also set the record for the most yards rushed by a quarterback in a single season. While Jackson has the yardage, Newton has the points. He holds the NFL quarterback record for the most career rushing touchdowns with 75.

Jackson threw a career-high 41 touchdown passes in the 2024 regular season.

CONSIDER THIS

Newton and Jackson are two of a small number of football players who have won both the Heisman Trophy and the NFL MVP award. Fewer than 10 players have won both top awards.

But being a quarterback isn't easy. Mistakes happen. Newton threw 130 interceptions and fumbled 67 times during his career in both the regular season and postseason. Jackson has already fumbled more often for a total of 70 times. But he has thrown only 56 interceptions so far.

Jackson faces pressure from a Kansas City Chiefs defender in 2024.

Despite his talent, Newton never won a Super Bowl.

Newton and Jackson's skills have helped their teams reach the playoffs multiple times. Newton led the Panthers to the playoffs four times, including one Super Bowl. Jackson has led the Ravens to the playoffs six times. Yet neither player has been able to lead their team to the ultimate prize: a Super Bowl win.

CHAPTER 4

Newton gets ready to receive his 2011 NFL Offensive Rookie of the Year award.

AND THE WINNER IS

So who wins this all-star smackdown? It is a tight matchup. Many people will have different opinions.

Newton and Jackson have proven their talents on the field. They are both Heisman Trophy winners. They both hold NFL rushing records. Newton was a First-Team All-Pro in 2015. The

First-Team All-Pro is a list that ranks the best NFL players in each position. Jackson was a First-Team All-Pro in 2019, 2023, and 2024.

Both players have earned plenty of awards. Newton was the NFL's Offensive Rookie of the Year in 2011 and the Offensive Player of the Year in 2015. He also was the league's MVP in 2015. Jackson has been the NFL MVP multiple times, winning in 2019 and 2023.

Jackson runs for a touchdown against the Houston Texans in 2024.

This is a smackdown of inches. But in the end, it goes to Lamar Jackson. He has more MVPs and All-Pro selections. He also has a higher completion percentage. Plus, Jackson is still out there playing and racking up points and awards. Maybe someday he will even win a Super Bowl ring.

What do you think? Think about each player's achievements. Consider their stats. Decide for yourself which all-star has what it takes to win this smackdown.

Newton narrowly avoids a tackle during a 2018 game against the Atlanta Falcons.

Jackson is known for his quick decisions and speed on the field.

SMACKDOWN BREAKDOWN

CAM NEWTON

Height: 6 feet 5 (2 m)
MVP awards: 1
First-Team All-Pro: 1
Pro Bowl selections: 3

LAMAR JACKSON

Height: 6 feet 2 (1.9 m)
MVP awards: 2
First-Team All-Pro: 3
Pro Bowl selections: 4

GLOSSARY

draft: when teams take turns picking new players

dual threat: a quarterback who can both throw and run the football

fumble: when a football player loses hold of the ball

Heisman Trophy: an award given every year to the best college football player in the country

interception: a pass caught by the defending team

opponent: a player on the other team

rookie: a player in their first year

running back: a football player whose main job is running with the ball

rush: to run the football forward on the field

sack: to tackle the quarterback behind the line of scrimmage

LEARN MORE

Adamson, Thomas K. *The Carolina Panthers*. Bellwether Media, 2024.

Britannica Kids: Baltimore Ravens
https://kids.britannica.com/students/article/Baltimore-Ravens/571000

Kiddle: Cam Newton Facts for Kids
https://kids.kiddle.co/Cam_Newton

Kiddle: National Football League Facts for Kids
https://kids.kiddle.co/National_Football_League

Leed, Percy. *Meet Lamar Jackson: Baltimore Ravens Superstar*. Lerner Publications, 2025.

Stewart, Mark. *The Baltimore Ravens*. Norwood House Press, 2025.

INDEX

PHOTO ACKNOWLEDGMENTS

Image credits: Kevin Hoffman/Getty Images, p. 4; Rob Carr/Getty Images, p. 5; Ronald C. Modra/Getty Images, p. 6; Rob Carr/Getty Images, p. 7; Darrell Walker/Icon Sportswire/Getty Images, p. 8; Todd Kirkland/Icon Sportswire/Getty Images, p. 9; Thomas B. Shea/Getty Images, p. 10; Billie Weiss/Getty Images, p. 11; Rich Graessle/Icon Sportswire/Getty Images, p. 12; Jonathan Newton/The Washington Post/Getty Images, p. 13; Rob Tringali/SportsChrome/Getty Images, p. 14; Kevin C. Cox/Getty Images, p. 15; Focus on Sport/Getty Images, p. 16; Nick Cammett/Diamond Images/Getty Images, p. 17; Todd Rosenberg/Getty Images, p. 18; Robin Alam/ISI Photos/Getty Images, p. 19; Justin K. Aller/Getty Images, p. 20; Rob Carr/Getty Images, p. 21; Rob Carr/Getty Images, p. 22; Kevin C. Cox/Getty Images, p. 23; Mike Coppola/Getty Images for Pepsi/Getty Images, p. 24; Patrick Smith/Getty Images, p. 25; Todd Kirkland/Icon Sportswire/Getty Images, p. 26; Michael Owens/Getty Images, p. 27; Patrick Smith/Getty Images, p. 28; Michael Owens/Getty Images, p. 29.

Cover: Scott Winters/Icon Sportswire/Newscom; Dannie Walls/Icon Sportswire/Newscom.